How to Stay Anonymous on the Internet

Disappearing from the Web

(Internet Security, Darknet)

By William Rowley

Copyright©2017 by William Rowley
All Rights Reserved

Copyright © 2017 by William Rowley

All rights reserved. No part of this publication may be reproduced, distributed, or transmitted in any form or by any means, including photocopying, recording, or other electronic or mechanical methods, without the prior written permission of the author, except in the case of brief quotations embodied in critical reviews and certain other noncommercial uses permitted by copyright law.

Table of Contents

Introduction	5
Chapter 1- Encrypting your Emails and Files	6
Chapter 2- Killing Cookies	17
Chapter 3- MAC (Media Access Control) Change	26
Chapter 4- Crypto Currencies	36
Chapter 5- Chain Proxies for Masking IP Addresses	51
Chapter 6- Downloading Torrents Anonymously	62
Conclusion	69

Disclaimer

While all attempts have been made to verify the information provided in this book, the author does assume any responsibility for errors, omissions, or contrary interpretations of the subject matter contained within. The information provided in this book is for educational and entertainment purposes only. The reader is responsible for his or her own actions and the author does not accept any responsibilities for any liabilities or damages, real or perceived, resulting from the use of this information.

The trademarks that are used are without any consent, and the publication of the trademark is without permission or backing by the trademark owner. All trademarks and brands within this book are for clarifying purposes only and are the owned by the owners themselves, not affiliated with this document. **

Introduction

Most people do not know that there might be an individual somewhere who might be spying them as they surf the Internet. There are various ways that a third party can spy the activities that you do online. However, it is possible for us to protect ourselves from such. This way, it will be possible for us to surf the Internet anonymously. This book guides you on how to stay anonymous whenever you are surfing the Internet. However, it is good for you to note that for you to stay anonymous online, you should use a wide variety of techniques, as a single technique is not enough. Enjoy reading!

Chapter 1- Encrypting your Emails and Files

True crypt is an open source tool which can help you to encrypt your data and stay anonymous online. True crypt is a powerful tool, and it offers you volume, partition, and a drive encryption, as well as the ability to set up other hidden volumes or an entire hidden OS. This means that in case you need to reveal your encryption password for any reason, the hidden volume will stay undetectable and encrypted inside your visible volume. This can be seen as a safe room kept within another safe room.

Begin by downloading True crypt from www.True crypt.org and then install it into your computer. The next step should involve the setting up of an already encrypted area which you will use so as to store your files. Begin by launching True crypt and then click on "Create Volume." Next, choose "Create an encrypted file container."

You will be provided with an option to enable you to create an hidden volume, and these have to be created inside a standard True crypt volume which is in existence, so you can select a Standard for now.

Next, click on "Select File," and then choose a location and some file name for the new True crypt container. However, avoid the use of a file name which already exists, otherwise, this will overwrite the old file by the new container.

Select your encryption, and then the hash algorithm. If you are a novice, it is advisable that you stick to the given defaults and then choose the size of the container plus some suitable and strong password. Lastly, you may be prompted to move the mouse randomly round your True crypt window for not less than 30 seconds. Note that the longer you take moving the mouse over the window, the stronger the encryption which will be created and your container will have been created.

If you need to use, then move back to the home screen for the True crypt and select any spare drive letter, then choose the container file from your Volume dropdown, and click on Mount. Type in your password and you will see the volume appear on the Windows Explorer like any other drive. Try to drag a file into this drive, and the file will be encrypted immediately and then added to your container. Try to open the file which has been encrypted and this will then decrypt in your RAM temporarily. When you are through with the container, click on Dismount, and you will see it disappear, and safely locked from any prying eyes.

There is much that you can be able to do from this point. It is possible for you to create some hidden volume inside the standard volume and the similar process we have followed for creating the container can be used for encrypting a partition or the whole of the OS.

Tor is an open and free virtual network which bounces communications all over the world so as to prevent the sites from learning one's physical location. Most security applications are based on the Tor technology, and a good example of this is the Tor browser. It was developed based on Firefox, meaning that it is easy for you to work with it, and for those who follow the instructions which are recommended, you will get the anonymity you have been yearning for.

If you need to setup this browser in your computer, you should first download its bundle from www.torproject.org and this will provide you with all the necessary tools. You can run the downloaded file, choose a location in which you will extract it, and then click on "Start Tor Browser." The setup process will automatically be done on your behalf, and once the installation and setup are done, the Tor browser will be launched for you. Just shut down the browser, and then disconnect your computer from the network.

Although the Tor browser is related to Firefox, there is still a huge difference, and your browsing experience won't be as usual. There are some plugins which are capable of revealing your identity as you surf the internet. In Tor, these plugins have been disabled by default, unlike in Firefox. However, it is good for you to note that the Tor browser will not be protecting the traffic which is getting into your computer. This is why you are discouraged from using other browsers such as Chrome.

Messaging

The use of tools for public key cryptography nowadays is not only for the IT experts, but more people from all over the world have begin to use tools such as OpenPGP so as to maintain secure communications online.

With PGP, one has to generate two keys. The public key is what can be shared with the others, as they can make use of this key for encrypting any messages which need your attention. The private key should be kept secret and safe; since it works together with the public key for unlocking the messages once they have arrived. When you have the public key only, it will be impossible for you to decrypt a message, and this can even be given to anyone despite your location or whether you have ever met or not. For this to work, both the sender and the receiver of the message must have installed the tool into their computers.

For Windows users, Gpg4win is good for you, and this is a suite that contains GnuPG and a few other tools and extensions, and a PDF for good Gpg4win Compendium. Gpg4win comes with all the tools you need for your use. It has plugins for Outlook, as well as an email client which is very much compatible with the keys which you generate.

For you to generate the pair of keys, you should run Kleopatra which is installed alongside the Gpg4win, and then click on File, New Certificate. Select the first option which pops up, then enter name and the email, and then click on Create Key.

The passphrase you choose is important, as the strength of this will determine the strength of the encryption. We recommend that you try and use a phrase which is at least four to five words long, and ensure that this is easy to remember. You can back up the newly created key pair in case you need to, then Export your certificate to some suitable folder on the PC. Once you open the certificate file, and you will get the public key in some text form.

That is the basic setup, but you should be aware that there is still more which you can do. The Gpg4win Compendium comes with a document which has walkthroughs for all, meaning that you should work through these examples until you are very confident enough to begin using OpenPGP together with your friends or relatives.

However, you should note that the Gpg4win tool does not handle instant messaging.

Disk Cleaning

An excellent disk cleaner is very essential for staying anonymous. A good example of such a tool is the BleachBit, which is a piece of software which can shred your files so as to prevent any recovery, and then overwrite your free disk space so as to hide the traces of the old files. Although you may think that you will not need to make use of the tool more often, remember that this tool hunts down and then automatically deletes any unnecessary files located anywhere on the hard disk, from the caches and the cookies to temporary folders belonging to thousands of applications.

In case your backups are growing, or in case you need to compress a disk image, the BleachBit tool is a quick means of maintaining a manageable size. The software can be downloaded from Bleachbit.sourceforge.net. You can then install the downloaded file into your computer and then run it. Any applications which are supported as well as the applications which will be deleted will be shown on the interface. Identify anything that you need to clean, but leave the ones you are not sure of. To see the amount of space that you will have cleaned up, just click on "Preview." Click on the "Clean" option so as to finish your job.

The other extra files can be found in the File dropdown menu. The Shred folders and Shred files commands will work by deleting and then overwriting the data which you have selected. The Wipe Free Space command works by going through the drive or the partition and then overwriting the files which were previously deleted by any of the software, meaning that it will not be easy to recover the files. Once this is done, the BleachBit will make an attempt to wipe the metadata about the files by filling the Master File Table of the Window.

Chapter 2- Killing Cookies

Cookies are used in browsers as they help them to load faster. When cookies are enabled on your browser, it will be possible for websites to remember you after visiting them and get your details such as passwords. Although this can be more useful, it is dangerous when it comes to maintaining your anonymity online. This is because they work by collecting and then storing data. With cookies, one can spy on you and learn the kind of person you are, what you like, and the time you spend while browsing online.

CCleaner is a tool which can help you to clean your cookies. The tool can help you to wipe out a lot of stuff. Browsers usually store web files on the system, so as to speed up the browsing in the future. Once you have revisited a site, it will load faster in case the images and the other files were cached on the system. Once you clear these files, you will have freed up more space and then improve your browsing privacy, which is good for your anonymity.

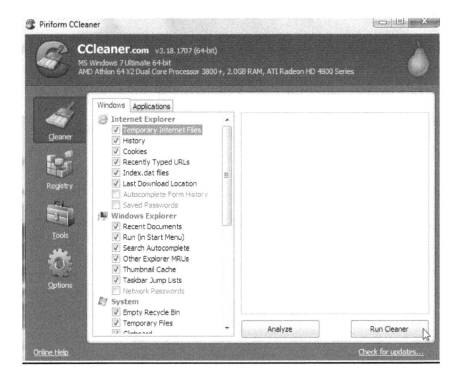

Once you erase the thumbnail cache which is under the Windows Explorer, you will have slowed things down and in any case you open a folder having numerous image files, some time will be taken so as to recreate the cache. If you clear it, you will not have freed up space, but you will have to recreate the cache at a later time.

There are other options which clear the most-recently-used lists (MRUs) in Windows and some other programs. Such lists do not occupy much space, but they can raise privacy concerns. If you have the most-recently-used list which you rely on, just be sure that you have unchecked it.

The CCleaner tool can also be used for cleaning up the cookies from your browser. The tools also allow one to retain some cookies, but since we need to maintain our anonymity online, we will have to clean all the cookies from the browser.

In case you find yourself logging into the favorite websites always after you run the CCleaner, just open the Cookies pane in the Options section. With the tool, it is also possible for you to do white listing. You just have to right click on the cookies pane and then select an Intelligent scan. The tool will automatically add the cookies for Hotmail, Google, and Yahoo Mail to the white list.

If you need to add a single cookie to the white list, you have to find it from the list of cookies and then click on the right arrow which is located next to it.

Although CCleaner includes a registry cleaner, we don't recommend that you run it. The Windows registry has thousands of the entries and removing a few hundreds of these will not offer an increase in the performance. The registry cleaner can accidentally remove the important registry values, meaning that you experience a risk with a little reward.

The CCleaner tool is very safe. However, it is good for you to ensure that you backup the changes which you make. The registry entries which you have deleted can be from the backup file whenever you encounter any problems.

The Startup panel located in the Tools section usually allows one to disable the programs which run automatically once the computer has started. If you need to avoid losing the auto start entry which can be very important, use the Disable option rather than the Delete option. One can easily re-enable the disabled auto start entry at a later time.

Once Windows or any other operating system has deleted a file, it does not wipe the file from the hard disk. The pointers to your files are deleted, while the operating system will mark the location of the file as a free space. With file recovery programs, you can scan the hard disk for the files, and, in case the operating system has not written over this area, you can recover your data. The CCleaner tool can help you protect against this happening by wiping your free space with the Drive Wiper tool.

It is a common belief that multiple passes will be needed if one wants to delete the files irrecoverably by use of the CCleaner. However, a single pass is enough for this. The tool can also help you to delete all the data on the disk. The CCleaner can also be made to wipe free space each time one runs it just by enabling the Wipe Free Space checkbox located under the Advanced in Cleaner section. Once you enable this option, you will make the CCleaner take longer so as to clean up the system, and this is why it is recommended that you leave this disabled.

Secure Deletion of Files

One can use the Disk Cleaner tool to delete each file securely from the disk. However, it is good for you to be aware that this will take a longer time than usual. This is the reason why the operating systems will never delete files by default. To improve your privacy, this option can be enabled from the settings tab.

Chapter 3- MAC (Media Access Control) Change

Each network interfaces, may it be Wi-Fi or wired, has a MAC address. This is just a serial number which comes with the network card from the vendor. The addresses are used for identification of communication between the network interfaces.

IP addresses usually tell you where you are on the Internet, but MAC addresses usually tell the device that you are using to connect to the network. Note that MAC addresses become useful only in a local network, but they are never sent to the Internet. With this kind of a private identifier, it will be impossible for you to stay anonymous on the Internet.

These calls for us to implement a technique which will help us conceal the identity of the MAC address of our network interfaces. This is called "MAC address spoofing." With a tool named "Tails," it is possible for one to change the MAC address of the network interface temporarily to some random values during the working session. This technique comes enabled by default in Tails.

There are different ways that one can look for MAC addresses of their network interface cards depending on the kind of operating system that you are using.

For Windows users, click on "Start" and then click on the "Run" option. On the dialog which appears, type "cmd" and then hit the enter key.

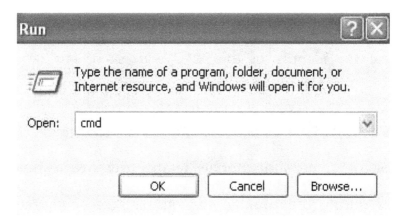

On the terminal which appears, type "ipconfig /all" and then hit the enter key. Look for the tag labeled "physical address" and then mark its corresponding value. That will be the MAC address of the interface, but ensure that you get this for the right network interface.

For users of Mac OS X, do the following to get the MAC address:

1) Open the *System Preferences*.

2) Choose the *AirPort* or the *Built-in Ethernet*, based on how you are able to access the network.

- In the case of Ethernet, click on *Advanced* and then navigate to the *Ethernet* tab. From the top, the Ethernet ID will be shown, and this will be the MAC address.

- For AirPort, click *Advanced* and navigate to the bottom of the page. You will be able to see the AirPort ID of the MAC address.

For Linux users, do the following:

1. **Obtain the** COMMAND SHELL. Based on the system, it might be named XTERM, TERMINAL, SHELL, COMMAND PROMPT, or anything similar. This can be

found under the APPLICATIONS > ACCESSORIES (or similar).

2. **Type in** /SBIN/IPCONFIG **and then press** ENTER. In case you are denied access, just enter SU –C "/SBIN/IPCONFIG" and then enter the root password if you are prompted.

3. **You can then look for the** HWADDR. This will be the MAC address.

To spoof the Mac address, you should use the network manager.

Windows

First, begin by launching the network manager. For users of Windows 8.1, you have to press the Windows Key + X and then click on the Device Manager. For users of Windows 7, just press the Windows key, and type "Device Manager" so as to search for this, and then click on the Device Manager. Identify the interface card which you need to change the settings of, and then right click on it. Click on Properties.

Click on the Advanced tab and then choose Network Address from the list. If you don't find this feature, just know that your network address is not capable of supporting this. Enable the value, and then type in the MAC address which you desire. Ensure that you don't use any characters such as colons for colons. Once done, click Ok. You will be done.

Linux

With modern versions of the Linux distributions such as Ubuntu, the Device Manager is used, and this provides us with a graphical interface through which we can be able to do this. For Ubuntu users, click on the network icon which is located on the top of the panel, and then click on Edit Connections. Identify the network connection which you need to modify, and then click on Edit. From the Ethernet tab, enter the new MAC addresses you wish to have under the "Cloned MAC address" and then save the changes you have made.

It is possible for us to do it in the old way. This way, you have to shut down the interface card, change the MAC address and then bring it up. Ensure that you have replaced the "eth0" with name of the network interface which you need to modify, and then enter the MAC address you desire to have. The following sequence of commands can be used for this purpose:

sudo ifconfig eth0 down

sudo ifconfig eth0 hw ether xx:xx:xx:xx:xx:xx

sudo ifconfig eth0 up

The necessary configuration file will have to be modified under the file /etc/network/interfaces.d/ or under /etc/network/interfaces file if you need the change to take effect anytime you boot the machine. In case you don't need it, the MAC address will have to be reset whenever you restart.

Mac OS X

The System Preferences panel for Mac OS X usually displays each of the network interface's MAC address. However, it doesn't allow you to make changes to it. A single command can help you to do this.

Launch the terminal window by pressing Command + Space and then type Terminal. You can then hit the enter key. Execute the command given below and ensure that you use the correct name for the network interface as well as the correct Mac address.

sudo ifconfig eno xx:xx:xx:xx:xx:xx

The eno should be replaced with the correct name for the interface as well as the MAC address. The name of the interface should be either eno or en1, and this can be determined by whether you need to change either the Wi-Fi network interface or the Ethernet network interface. In case you don't know the name for the network interface, you can execute the "ifconfig" command, and this will help you know the names of the available network interfaces.

Note that the change will be temporary and it will only take effect after you reboot the system. If you need to make the new MAC address to be permanent, then you will have to implement a script which will implement it after each reboot of the system.

If you need to verify that the change took effect, you can run a command which shows the network connection details and then check which MAC address the network interface will report afterwards. For Windows users, run the "**ipconfig /all**" command from the Command Prompt window. For Linux or Mac OS X users, run the "**ifconfig**" command.

In case you need to make a change on the MAC address of your router, this option can be found on the web interface of the router.

Chapter 4- Crypto Currencies

Crypto currencies can help one to browse the Internet anonymously. They have been used by most drug dealers for online transactions.

When Bitcoin is used in the normal manner, it is more of pseudonymous currency, but not an anonymous one. One can download some piece of software and then install it on a computer to be able to use Bitcoin. Since it is decentralized and a peer-to-peer system, one doesn't need to register for an account with any company or provide any of their personal details except in cases where one chooses to do so. After you get a wallet, you are able to create an address which will effectively become your own identity within the network. This will already give you an enhanced level of privacy as compared to the other online payment systems, since you will be able to use the network anonymously.

Bitcoin also has another side. Since the transactions have to be confirmed by your network, and the transaction history has to be shared between all the participants, a public record for all the transactions exists, and this can be accessed by anybody. This is something which happens in the Bitcoin network.

This means that although the personal identity as owner of the wallet may not be available in the public domain, all the transactions that you take part in will be in the public knowledge. This is a problem to anyone who is looking for how to stay anonymous online, since there is a way one can associate the wallet links that you make use of to your personal identity.

Most exchanges dealing with the buying and selling of digital currency usually rely on centralized service providers in need of at least identity information from the customer before the service can be used. This is an example of a service which makes use of Bitcoin, but requires identity information and there exists many other such services.

Once you analyze the activity that is visible to anyone on the public block chain, the observer can be able to link their personal identity to all the wallets which you use, hence the whole of the transaction history. In such a way, Bitcoin may be less secure compared to a bank account.

However, there is a way for one to use Bitcoin in an anonymous manner.

Disposable Addresses

The majority of beginners will do it by downloading the wallet software, then create one or two address, then continue using the addresses for some extended time. If you need privacy, it is not the right way for you to make use of your wallet. If you make more use of an address, it will be easier for an observer to create a profile of the activities you perform, may it be advertising or a more sinister purpose, even linking an activity to the personal identity.

The Bitcoin addresses will not be created so as to stay in permanent locations for each task that you do. However, it enhances your financial privacy whenever you view the addresses as disposable invoices. It is recommended that you create an address whenever you have received Bitcoin specifically for the purpose, and never make use of that address afterwards.

For those having a desktop wallet on their computer, you should be in a position to create any addresses without facing any problem, no matter the number that you create, all the old addresses will be in a position to receive payment whenever somebody sends you some money by use of an old address they have on the file for you.

Most of today's wallets have solved this problem, as they create a new address for you whenever you are to receive a payment and this is done automatically, but it is good for you to know that this issue exists.

Bitcoin Mixing

A mixing service can also help you to enhance your anonymity when browsing online. This service can be used whenever you need to send some payment to someone, whenever you need to send some coins to your own wallet, or when you need to send your coins to another address which belongs to you.

In this case, the anonymity is achieved by mixing your coins together with several other coins from the other side's before you can send these to the other side. This means that it will become impossible or difficult for any observer to link the specific payments into a mixing service to specific payments which are coming out of the mixing service.

A good example which offers such a service is the CoinMixer.se but you can also Google for several others which are very helpful. However, before going for one, it will be good for you to check for the reviews and see how they have been written. There is a possibility that some will steal your coins.

How to Buy and Sell Coins Anonymously

Most people do not know how to buy and sell bitcoins anonymously so that their activities are not linked to your real identity.

The greatest risk lies at the time of buying the coins, as the digital activities are usually associated with one's personal identity, since the majority of the sites need you to perform verification of the identity and then provide your ID documents so as to do the purchase. This usually helps them to avoid any prosecution due to the laws regarding money laundering. For one who needs to stay anonymous as they use bitcoins, this is a very important action.

The following actions can help you to maintain your anonymity when buying and selling bitcoins:

1. By use of a peer-to-peer exchange in which you will be able to buy and then sell with the other individual users instead of a company provides one with better privacy compared to the use of a central service.

    Let us discuss some of the exchanges in which one is able to buy and sell their bitcoins without necessarily having to provide their identity details or verify to ensure that they are correct:

- Bitsquare- this exchange is totally decentralized, and the trade is done directly without having to use any central service provider. You have to download some piece of P2P software instead of having to go to a website. Once Bitsquare has been opened, it will create your "hidden service" on TOR using your .onion address, and route everything through such a good established privacy service so as to hide the IP address which trackers can use for identifying you. You are not required to do any registration nor provide your username. However, you are expected to provide a small security deposit which is of 0.01 bitcoin and you get it back after you have made the trade or after you cancel the offer, meaning that if you need to buy the first bitcoin, you should first get one by use of other mechanisms. It is one of the best ways to trade coins anonymously. However, the fixed fees you have to pay means that this option can be expensive when small amounts are to be traded.

- MultiSigna- This is the technology for several exchanges, which means that one doesn't need to trust the coins to the exchange for safe keeping, or even depend on the exchange for keeping the internal books accurately since everything lays on the blockchain. As a user of the defunct exchanges such as Mt Gox will attest, it gives us a big bonus when it comes to terms of security, and makes these more directly peer-to-peer and decentralized than the other options. The fees usually start at a standard 0.5%, but for regular trader and then progress through "user levels," you are able to take advantage of the reduced fees.

- LocalBitcoins- this is a very popular peer-to-peer service used for the buying and selling of coins, and it is operational in different countries in the world. As you use the site, you will have an option to provide your identity information or bypass this. The other users will have the option for dealing with the anonymous users or require them to provide their identity information. The majority of the users may need some identity information, through the ID verification system of the site or privately over the chat so as to protect against fraud as well as government investigation. This method also provides you with a mechanism for you to do any anonymous trade that you may need.

- Coinffeine- This is a peer-to-peer and decentralized exchange. The only payment method provided currently is OKPay, and it has own identification requirements.

However, you are not expected to share your personal information via Coinffeine itself, and your additional payment methods are an added advantage to you in the future.

2. Whenever one is making a purchase on LocalBitcoins, the users who are concerned about privacy have to make their payment in cash. This becomes important when one is making a high volume of purchases since the volume can trigger an investigation by the bank. However, this is not of much importance to those making small transactions. This can be done either by an in-person trade in which you will meet up with the person or through a "cash deposit" in which you will go to a branch of the seller's bank and then deposit the money directly into the account they own. Sign up and then click on "buy bitcoins," and underneath the list of top offers, a link saying "Show More" will be visible and it will show you the list of the payment methods you can

choose from, meaning if you click on "cash deposit." only the offers from the users who need to sell coins through the method will be visible.

3. The LocalBitcoins site has an ID verification system, but this is optional. Some of the sellers will need this, but others will not need it. In the case of some sellers, you may be asked to send a copy of your ID to them via a private message. Generally, it is better for you to provide your ID to an individual rather than uploading it to the main site. However, it is possible that some people will not feel comfortable with this. It is good for each of the sellers to list the particular requirement in their advertisement, and one can send a message to them before opening the trade so as to obtain more information about policies, meaning that it's not difficult for one to "shop around" for the right seller.

Stealth Addresses

This is a new feature that allows users to be able to generate a new public address so as to represent a regular Bitcoin address. It means that one can send money to the new stealth address and no one will know the real destination of these funds. There is no need for a wallet that supports such a feature so as to use it, and the adoption of this has not been wide. But it is good for you to try it and **Dark wallet** is a good one for one to get started. This is a browser wallet that works like an extension for Google Chrome and it has stealth addresses and other privacy features.

Taint Analysis

For those who have ever used the coin mixer, just check how good their privacy services perform with taint analysis. This will show the addresses that have sent coins to the address, and it is a good way for you to see whether mixing services are doing it to your expectations.

There are different services out there, and if one does not satisfy your needs, it will be good for you to go for another service. A Blockchain website can help you to do a taint analysis.

Chapter 5- Chain Proxies for Masking IP Addresses

A proxy is just a server which allows a client to establish a connection to it and then forward its traffic. It allows a specific "layer" of protection as it masks the IP address. An **IP address** can be used to learn your location and track you on the Internet, thus eliminating any form of anonymity that you may have.

Proxy Chains is just a cool tool which allows one to chain multiple proxies so as to establish a connection to each other and wrap the program of choice and then connect you to the Internet. This will mask the IP with many other layers, and this can be a good tool when one is practicing anonymity.

To make use of this, follow the steps given below:

1. You should begin by downloading Proxy Chains.

   Download Proxy Chains and then install it into your computer. Once you have downloaded the package, open the terminal and then execute the following sequence of commands:

   To extract the package, use the following command:

   sudo tar -zxvf <package name>

   You can then change your directory and perform the configuration as follows:

cd <proxychains directory> && ./configure

You can then go ahead to compile and then configure the source code:

sudo make

The installation of Poxy Chains can then be done by executing the following command:

sudo make install

You can then configure and make use of Proxy Chains:

You can use Proxy Chains and Tor so as to anonymize any attacks that you need to carry out. Tor is a free software program and open network which helps one to defend against any form of a network surveillance which threatens the personal freedom and one's privacy, relationships, and confidential business activities, and the state security which is referred to as traffic analysis.

Begin by installing Tor by executing the following command:

sudo apt-get install tor

You can then edit the file /etc/proxychains.conf by adding the following line to it:

socks4 127.0.0.1 9050

After that, it will be possible for you to run your examples anonymously. It is possible for you to configure your browser so that you will be able to surf the Internet without the use of proxy chains. You should begin by editing the connection settings so as to add a manual proxy. It will then be in a position to hide your connections.

Anonymous Port Scanning

Nmap, which is a utility which helps in network discovery and for security auditing can help one to stay anonymous during the scanning of ports. The Proxy Chains utility can help us achieve this in the Tor network.

Now that you have Tor and Proxy Chains already installed, it is time for you to install Nmap. The following command can help you to achieve this:

$ sudo apt-get install nmap

Note that Proxy Chains comes readily configured to make use of the Tor network. If you need to verify whether this has been set, you just have to open the file /etc/proxychains.conf. The last two lines of the file should be as follows:

[ProxyList]

add the proxy here ...

meanwile

defaults set to "tor"

socks4 127.0.0.1 9050

The anonymous port scanning can be enabled by running the following command via the Tor network:

$ proxychains nmap -sT -PN -n -sV -p 80,443,21,22 217.xx.xx.xx

ProxyChains-3.1 (http://proxychains.sf.net)

Starting Nmap 6.00 (http://nmap.org) at 2014-03-24 17:34 EET

|S-chain|-<>-127.0.0.1:9050-<><>-217.xx.xx.xx:443-<><>-OK

|S-chain|-<>-127.0.0.1:9050-<><>-217.xx.xx.xx:21-<><>-OK

|S-chain|-<>-127.0.0.1:9050-<><>-217.xx.xx.xx:80-<><>-OK

|S-chain|-<>-127.0.0.1:9050-<><>-217.xx.xx.xx:22-<--denied

Nmap **scan report for 217.xx.xx.xx**

Host **is up (0.14s latency).**

PORT   STATE   SERVICE VERSION

21/tcp open   ftp   Pure-FTPd

22/tcp closed ssh

80/tcp open   http   Apache **httpd 2.2.26 ((CentOS))**

443/tcp open   ssl/http Apache **httpd 2.2.26 ((CentOS))**

From the scan log, you can see the chain moving the Tor proxy which is 127.0.0.1:9050 to the scanned host.

Most probably, it may happen that the scan will fail simply because the Tor endpoints will have been blocked. The only solution to such a problem is by addition of a public proxy server which is common to the chain.

To do this, we have to edit the "/etc/proxychains.con" file, and then add some new entry to the end of the [ProxyList] as shown below:

[ProxyList]
add proxy here ...
meanwile
defaults set to "tor"
socks4 127.0.0.1 9050
socks4 115.71.237.212 1080

It is good for you to ensure that the option for "random option" has been disabled. The new chain will then be going through the Tor proxy which is 127.0.0.1:9050 to a public proxy server, which is 115.71.237.212:1080, and lastly to the scanned host. This is shown below:

```
$ proxychains nmap -sT -PN -n -sV -p 21 217.xx.xx.xx
```

ProxyChains-3.1 (http://proxychains.sf.net)

Starting Nmap 6.00 (http://nmap.org) at 2014-03-25 11:05 EET

|S-chain|-<>-127.0.0.1:9050-<>-115.71.237.212:1080-<><>-217.xx.xx.xx:21-<><>-OK

|S-chain|-<>-127.0.0.1:9050-<>-115.71.237.212:1080-<><>-217.xx.xx.xx:21-<><>-OK

Nmap scan report for 217.xx.xx.xx

Host is up (1.2s latency).

PORT   STATE SERVICE VERSION

21/tcp open ftp   Pure-FTPd

Note that in this section, Nmap has been run together with the following options:

- -sT- this is for a full TCP connection scan.

- -PN- for not performing the host discovery.

- -n- never to perform a DNS resolution so as to prevent the DNS leaks.

- -sV- this will determine the service version/info.

- -p- this is for port scanning.

If you need to prevent the DNS leaks, you can make use of the "tor-resolve" command for resolving a host name to an IP address through the Tor network. This is shown below:

$ tor-resolve google.com

Chapter 6- Downloading Torrents Anonymously

It is easy for one to download torrents, but for one to do it anonymously, some extra steps are needed. However, these extra steps are not hard for anyone, and they are worth it for one to do them.

The best approach to this is to make use of a reliable torrent VPN which does not keep logs. Note that any interaction on the Internet, such as torrent file-sharing as well as downloading, involves sharing the IP ADDRESS of your device and the unique online digital fingerprint. In case you fail to take steps to hide the IP address, the torrent downloading activities you perform can be easily traced to you.

For snoops to detect the IP address you are using and then track you down, they only have to share a torrent like you and monitor the activities of the swarm torrent. It means that for you to download the torrents anonymously you should have to hide the IP address and the outside parties will not snoop on, detect, or even monitor the activities you perform on torrent.

The following are some of the actions that a strong and reliable torrent VPN will do:

1. **Hide the true IP address.**

2. Use a **strong encryption** so as to scramble the torrent traffic.

3. Keep **no logs** of the activities you perform.

A reliable VPN will act like a **shield,** and it will **protects** the torrent activities you perform from being snooped on either by your ISP in need to throttle and shape the bandwidth or by an outsider eavesdropping on the connection so as to monitor your downloads. Although nothing will ever offer a 100% GUARANTEE of complete anonymity, such a combination of the features will make it all but it will be impossible for the snoops to detect the true IP address you are using, monitor the activities you perform, and track you down.

We will discuss how one is able to download the torrents in an anonymous manner. It is recommended that one should use an anonymizing torrent VPN service AND an IP address protection tool whenever they are sharing and downloading torrents.

The first step should be to start Anonymous Torrent VPN or Proxy. Note that the use of a special TORRENT ANONYMIZING SERVICE is the best way for anyone to hide their IP address. It means either the torrent-friendly VPN or the BitTorrent proxy. Let us focus on the torrent VPNs since they are versatile and they offer a better value for your money.

Once you enable the torrent VPN, note that the ISP will only be in a position to see your traffic in an encrypted manner. It will also be in a position to view the amount of data that you are downloading, but they will not be able to know what you are downloading. In the case of the outside snoops, they will not be in a position to monitor or eavesdrop on your torrent activities since they will not be in a position to attribute the activities of torrent to the real IP address you are using.

The Connection

Regardless of the anonymizing torrent VPN which you decide to make use of, ensure that you have connected it before you can begin to download or share any torrents. It will also be good for you to enable any of the "Advanced Settings" which your torrent VPN Provider may support.

For you to disconnect from the VPN, you just have to click on "Disconnect." After the disconnection is done, carefully note the masked IP address as this will be needed in the future. Note that the masked IP address is the IP address which the torrent VPN provider has assigned to you for the session. This one can easily be determined. A good torrent VPN provider will show this to the right in the VPN app or once you hover your mouse over the VPN section of the system tray. If this doesn't happen, it will be good for you to change the VPN provider.

Next, launch the IP Address protection tool that you are using. A good example of such a tool is the PeerBlock. It is not a must for one to use such a tool for them to stay anonymous when making torrent downloads. However, for those using such tools, they will be protected against any connections from a suspicious IP address. The IP protection tool is just an additional layer of protection which helps to protect your privacy regardless of whether or not you are using an anonymizing torrent VPN.

For Windows users, PeerBlock is the best one for you. The tool acts as firewall software, but it goes one step further to filter IP addresses which try to establish a connection to you against some specialized BLACKLISTS which have been compiled by torrent enthusiasts.

The blacklists PeerBlock will allow you to choose from include the ones protecting you from the IP addresses which are associated with spammers, spyware, snoops, governments, educational institutions, and anti-torrent elements.

You can then go ahead and confirm the IP address that the Torrent app is currently transmitting. At this point, go ahead and then start your Torrent app. Check for the IP address which is being transmitted by the Torrent app. This calls for you to do a check on this, and ensure that the check is specifically designed for torrents. With this, you will be sure that no one will know your true IP address. Once you are sure of this, it will be okay for you to go ahead and begin to download and share the torrents anonymously.

Whenever you are visiting torrent indexes as well as other websites which are related to this, it will be good for you to ensure that you stay anonymous. Some people will forget this and protect their IP address only when they are downloading the torrents but this is not recommended. You should look for mechanisms on how to stay protected against traffic analysis. This will ensure that you are anonymous when downloading the torrents.

Conclusion

We have come to the end of this guide. There are many ways that your identity can leak when you are surfing the Internet. For you to stay anonymous, you have to encrypt the files and emails which you send over the Internet. This way, no one will know the contents of your emails and the files you are transmitting online. Cookies, which are usually enabled on the browser, are a risk to anonymity.

They work by collecting information from your computer, and they can send the same information to a third party. They are the ones responsible for password remembrance when you login to some accounts online. With these enabled on the browser, it is hard for one to stay anonymous.

These calls are for you to kill the cookies on your browser. Any device that you use to surf the Internet has a MAC (Media

Access Address) which is unique to that device. This address can be used to trace the activities that you perform online back to you. A technique called MAC address spoofing helps to protect you from this. With this, your device is assigned a fake MAC address, meaning that no one will be able to know the real MAC address of your device, and you will stay anonymous while surfing the Internet. The fact is that for one to stay anonymous online, a single technique is not enough. This should involve a combination of multiple factors. I hope all the techniques discussed in this book have been helpful to you!

Printed in the USA
CPSIA information can be obtained
at www.ICGtesting.com
CBHW051308221024
16235CB00016B/148